# Grace

## For the Writer's Journey

*A six-week study to discover and partner with God's unique grace for you as His writer.*

Written by Janice Buswell & Laurel Thomas
From the Experience Writing 2025 Grace Conference

Grace for the Writer's Journey
Copyright © 2025 Experience Writing, LLC
All rights reserved.

Published by Experience Writing

Printed in the United States of America. All rights reserved under United States and International Copyright Law. Contents and/or cover may not be reproduced in whole or in part in any form without the express written consent of the author or publisher.

Requests for permission should be submitted in writing to:
Experience Writing, LLC, 7331 S. Olympia Ave., #306, Tulsa, OK, 74132

Scriptures in this book are quoted from the following translations:

Scripture quotations marked as NKJV are taken from the New King James Version®. Copyright © 1982 by Thomas Nelson. Used by permission. All rights reserved.

Scripture quotations marked TPT are from The Passion Translation®. Copyright © 2017, 2018, 2020 by Passion & Fire Ministries, Inc. Used by permission. All rights reserved. ThePassionTranslation.com. All Scripture quotations are from The Passion Translation®. Copyright © 2017, 2018, 2020 by Passion & Fire Ministries, Inc. Used by permission. All rights reserved. ThePassionTranslation.com.

Scripture quotations marked (ESV) are from the ESV® Bible (The Holy Bible, English Standard Version®), © 2001 by Crossway, a publishing ministry of Good News Publishers. ESV Text Edition: 2025. The ESV text may not be quoted in any publication made available to the public by a Creative Commons license. The ESV may not be translated in whole or in part into any other language. Used by permission. All rights reserved."

Scripture quotations marked MSG are taken from *THE MESSAGE*, copyright © 1993, 2002, 2018 by Eugene H. Peterson. Used by permission of NavPress. All rights reserved. Represented by Tyndale House Publishers, Inc.

Scripture quotations marked NIV are taken from THE HOLY BIBLE, NEW INTERNATIONAL VERSION®, NIV® Copyright © 1973, 1978, 1984, 2011 by Biblica, Inc.® Used by permission. All rights reserved worldwide.

Scripture quotations marked AMPC are taken from the Amplified® Bible (AMPC), Copyright © 1954, 1958, 1962, 1964, 1965, 1987 by The Lockman Foundation. Used by permission. [lockman.org](lockman.org)"

Scripture quotations that are unspecified are paraphrases by the authors.

ISBN 978-1-951830-06-9

# Small Group Suggestions

## Welcome, Writer!

This workbook is designed to help you and your writing friends discover or recover the unique gift God's given you as a writer by learning to actively partner with His grace for you in your growing relationship with Him. As you walk together through the next six weeks, you will have the opportunity to...

- Clarify your God-given story.
- Identify your unique audience.
- Pinpoint where you may have gotten stuck.
- Strategize your next steps forward.

All of this will take place in the context of your deepening relationship with God and your fellow writers.

WHY IS THIS A GROUP STUDY? - You can do this study on your own, however a great deal of benefit comes from back and forth discussion. This study is suited to speak to diverse groups with members of all backgrounds, ages, and experience levels. The content centers around our shared call as God's writers to be gatekeepers of His glory.

We can all learn from each other regardless of age, experience, or genres, and I encourage facilitators not to give preference to opinions based on the experience level of the sharer. Instead, keep your eyes on where God is at work and what He is doing in the lives of each of the individuals present. It is amazing how He can cross-pollinate us for greater fruitfulness as we honor and love one another through our unique journeys.

GROUP STRUCTURE SUGGESTIONS - Size. This study is suited to a group of around 4-10. Although, if you have experience facilitating groups, you could easily manage the content with a group of 15.

Structure. This study is composed of six lessons. Five of the six lessons include a video component, and all six lessons have a corresponding group workshop. The lesson videos are available on expwriting.gumroad.com/l/grace. Or you can use the QR code below.

Each lesson, with its videos, outlines, and activities, is meant to take 90 minutes of time and can be done individually in preparation for the group workshops. Each group workshop, also designed to take 90 minutes, consists of writing and discussion components. A helpful breakdown of timing and discussion questions is provided in each workshop section. One note: the Finding Grace lesson is unique in that its workshop is designed to move the group into a time of structured fellowship and prayer.

Frequency. We recommend a six week study that includes 90 minutes of personal preparation to study each lesson followed later in the week by a 90 minute group workshop meeting. However, if you prefer to view the lesson videos together, an every-other-week or monthly meeting of three hours might suit better. Feel free to adapt the format to your group's needs.

FOR FACILITATORS - We do recommend there is a designated facilitator for group workshop to help everyone get the most out of the experience. If you want to be a facilitator, each group workshop section in this workbook has designated writing, discussion, and occasionally reading sections to help you facilitate your group. Each section also has a suggested time duration to help you make it through the material within a 90 minute meeting. These suggestions aren't rigid! Be sure to be sensitive to any work the Lord may be doing in your group as you facilitate the discussions.

ONE CRITICAL NOTE - The biggest key to success in this study will be your willingness as a facilitator or group member to commit to pray weekly for each of the members of the group. God is the one who ultimately opens and connects hearts and who unveils His designs for our lives. As you pray over your fellow group members, it will create space for Him to speak and prepare your minds and hearts to receive.

We also encourage you to open each session with a brief prayer asking for His Spirit to fill you with His wisdom and love. Then close it by praying briefly together—for one another—to lift up any prayer needs that arose during the group workshop. There is nothing that knits our hearts to our Heavenly Father or to one another like prayer does.

I hope you enjoy this dive into the rich treasures of His heart as you walk together through these lessons. I trust you will gain clarity about who you are as His writer and His unique call for you in this season. He is our perfect teacher and the only source of all true creativity and inspiration.

Blessings and grace,

**Janice Buswell**
*Co-Founder of Experience Writing*

# Table of Contents

Small Group Suggestions ............................................................................................................3

## Grace for the Gatekeeper
- Lesson #1..............................................................................................................................9
- Workshop #1 ......................................................................................................................15

## Finding Grace
- Lesson #2............................................................................................................................21
- Workshop #2 *(Finding Grace Mingle)*............................................................................29

## Grace to be Untethered: An Invitation to Dance
- Lesson #3 ...........................................................................................................................33
- Workshop #3 .....................................................................................................................39

## Comfort for the Writer's Soul
- Lesson # ..............................................................................................................................45
- Workshop #4 .....................................................................................................................51

## Grace for Identity—Unearthing Treasure in Ourselves through Community
- Lesson #5 ...........................................................................................................................59
- Workshop #5 .....................................................................................................................65

## Next Steps
- Lesson #6 ...........................................................................................................................71
- Workshop #6 .....................................................................................................................75

Resources..................................................................................................................................77
About the Co-Authors.............................................................................................................79

# LESSON ONE
## Grace for the Gatekeeper

By Laurel Thomas

*B*ecoming a gatekeeper is more than a concept. As writers and creatives, we are called to an extraordinary life. Discover how your heart and words unite to open doors of freedom for others!

**AS WRITERS:**
**WHAT was the role of a gatekeeper? DO they still exist?**
**IF SO, WHAT does that mean for us, as writers?**

**Old Testament:**
Gatekeepers in the Old Testament were Levites called to fulfill a specific role in protecting and caring for the Temple. The role of gatekeeper was generational and considered a holy calling.

**Historical:**
A gatekeeper was positioned at heavy gates inside a walled city. His vigilance was essential to the protection of the city. If invaders approached without an alarm, they could breach the walls and take the city. A vigilant gatekeeper was key to the defense and protection of the city. The gatekeeper also gave access, especially to traders in desert cities whose caravans brought goods into an area that was cut off by miles of desert.

**HOW am I a gatekeeper?**

**WHY does it matter?**

**DEFINING THE CALL:**
1. **A HOLY CALLING.**

2. **VIGILANCE is required.**

3. **A VOICE that MUST be heard.**

4. **ACCESS to needed supply.**

**UNLIKELY GATEKEEPERS!**
Rahab, from the book of Joshua, was an unlikely gatekeeper. The condition of her heart—regardless of her circumstances—opened her eyes to see the reality of the King of kings and Lord of lords.
Her FAITH and OBEDIENCE opened an impossible door to the Promised Land for God's people.
Her actions were BOLD and courageous.

**\*We are keepers of DOORS that release Him to the world. Our faith to move forward opens the ways for others!**

**JOSHUA 1:5-6** – Just as I've been with Moses, so I will be with you. Be strong and courageous, for you will give this people possession of the land I promised them.

## DOOR:

A door is a means of access or participation. It is an opportunity.
That access can be locked by lack of knowledge or even demonic resistance.

Our job is to open doors to reveal His goodness, grace and opportunity. We are invited by His Spirit to release understanding and generosity. Perhaps in ways and in places it has not been experienced before.

I hold in My hands living understanding, courage, and strength. I empower kings to reign and rulers to make just laws. I empower princes to rise and take dominion, and generous ones to govern the earth. **Proverbs 8:14-15** *(TPT)*

*We don't need perfection, but we do need surrender to Him. Surrender of expectations and self-will. And lots of forgiveness/repentance on a regular basis!

*We have faith that brokenness doesn't disqualify us.

**SPRINGS OF LIFE –** Let the Spirit of the Lord help unclog any blockages/stones.
Pay attention to the welfare of your innermost being, for from there flows the wellspring of life.
**Proverbs 4:23** *(TPT)*

## *Grace for the Assignment and the Obstacles
Definition of grace – His ability empowering our ability

## 2 CORINTHIANS 12:9
My grace is always more than enough for you, and My power finds its full expression in your weakness. (Passion Translation)

## 2 CORINTHIANS 12:9-10
Once I heard that, I was glad to let it happen. I quit focusing on the handicap and began appreciating the gift. It was a case of Christ's strength moving in on my weakness. Now I take limitations in stride, and with good cheer...I just let Christ take over! (The Message)

## INTERACTIVE EXERCISE:

PRAY for healing – spirit, soul, and body. How does my faith and obedience to His assignment open doors for others?

# Additional Notes

# WORKSHOP ONE
## Grace for the Gatekeeper

*L*et's dive in and discover the "what," "why," and "who" of your call to write, as well as what's held you back from that call and the keys to overcome!

## YOUR CALL
WRITING SECTION (10min)

My Call from God as a Writer...
*What do you feel called to write? What story, message, or themes are burning in your heart?*

_____
_____
_____
_____
_____
_____
_____

Blockers...
*What top three things have kept me from writing?*
1)_____
2)_____
3)_____

## Roots...
*What is the root of each blocker? (The reason behind the blocker!)*
1)_____
2)_____
3)_____

## How to Remove the Roots...
1)_____
_____
2)_____
_____
3)_____
_____

## *DISCUSSION SECTION (30min)*
- *What's your call from God as a writer?*
- *What's your top blocker, its root, & your plan to remove it?*

# YOUR READERS
## *WRITING SECTION (5min)*

## Who God Wants to Reach on the Other Side...
*Who is waiting for your message on the other side of what's stopped you? Describe them and the change your story will make in their lives...*

Who needs your story?_____
_____
_____

What change will it make for them?_____
_____
_____

*Is there someone who comes to mind who represents that group of readers?*
_____

**The Role of Love.** It's hard to finish what's not motivated by love. But love never fails. Love is not always an emotion. It's also a choice.
_____
_____
_____
_____

*DISCUSSION SECTION (20min)*
- *Summarize: Who needs your story and what change will it make in their lives?*

# YOUR GATE
*WRITING SECTION (5min)*

Guarding Your Call
*Becoming the Gatekeeper of your heart. "Guard your heart for out of it flow the issues of life..." –* **Proverbs 4:23**

How can I stand as Gatekeeper over my heart?
- Maintain Clear Vision.
    - Know Your Why/Your Call
    - Know Who Needs Your Story
- Turn Weakness into Strength.
    - Use the word of God and scripture daily to replace lies and fears.

My Plan

_____
_____
_____
_____
_____

*DISCUSSION SECTION (20min)*
- *How do you plan to uproot your biggest blocker?*

# Friends Met @ Meeting #1

NAME:_____

EMAIL:_____PHONE:_____

NOTES:_____

_____

_____

_____


NAME:_____

EMAIL:_____PHONE:_____

NOTES:_____

_____

_____

_____


NAME:_____

EMAIL:_____PHONE:_____

NOTES:_____

_____

_____

_____


NAME:_____

EMAIL:_____PHONE:_____

NOTES:_____

_____

_____

_____

# LESSON TWO
# *Finding Grace*
## By Janice Buswell

*Learning to partner with the grace of God is a game-changer when it comes to answering your call as a writer. This session will give you a roadmap to discover and embrace the grace God has provided for you!*

## What Does Grace Have to Do with Writing?

*"For though I am the least of the apostles, this grace was given me: to make known the mystery of the Gospel to the Gentiles..." – Ephesians 3:8*

There is nothing we do _____ the grace of God.

*Ugandan Greeting ~ "Praise God! He's given me another day!"*

It's all about _____.

## What is Grace?

- Grace is very _____.

- Grace is the _____ of God to do the _____ of God.

- It's only when we learn to _____ with God's grace that we enter into His _____.

*For it is by free grace (God's unmerited favor) that you are saved (delivered from judgment and made partakers of Christ's salvation) through [your] faith. And this [salvation] is not of yourselves [of your own doing, it came not through your own striving] but it is the gift of God; Not because of works [not the fulfillment of the Law's demands], lest any man should boast ... For we are God's [own] handiwork (His workmanship), recreated in Christ Jesus, [born anew] ... -* ***Ephesians 2:8-10** (AMPC)*

- Salvation is the most _____ thing that will ever happen in a person's life. And it's accomplished _____. But salvation is not where God's grace _____.

*For we are God's [own] handiwork (His workmanship), recreated in Christ Jesus, [born anew], that we **may do those good works** which God predestined (planned beforehand) for us [taking paths which He prepared ahead of time], that we should walk in them [living the good life which He prearranged and made ready for us to live]. –* ***Ephesians 2:10** (AMPC)*

- Our works will never _____ grace, because His grace is what _____ to do any _____.

## Partnering with Grace – Step #1

*But by the grace of God I am what I am, and His grace toward me was not for nothing. In fact, I worked harder than all of them though it was not really I, but the grace of God which was with me. –* ***1 Corinthians 15:10** (AMPC)*

- Actively partnering with God's _____ is really partnership with God _____.

*Therefore, my dear ones, as you have always obeyed ... so now, not only ... in my presence but much more because I am absent, work out ... your own salvation with reverence and awe and trembling ... [Not in your own strength] for it is God Who is all the while effectually at work in you [energizing and creating in you the power and desire], both to will and to work for His good pleasure and satisfaction and delight.* – **Philippians 2:12-13** *(AMPC)*

- We do not realize the _____ God avails to us to _____ the work He's given. He withholds nothing. And if He did not spare His own Son, will He not along with Him give us all things? (Romans 8:32) But first, we have to...

1) _____

    o We have to _____ for grace.

    o We have not because we _____.

*Since then we have a great high priest who has passed through the heavens, Jesus, the Son of God, let us hold fast our confession. For we do not have a high priest who is unable to sympathize with our weaknesses, but one who in every respect has been tempted as we are, yet without sin. Let us then with confidence draw near to the throne of grace, that we may receive mercy and find grace to help in time of need.* – **Hebrews 4:14-16** *(ESV)*

   o Historically, people always approached a throne with a _____.

   o We're told to _____ approach the throne of grace in time of need. Why?

   o God wants to _____ with us.

   o Partnership requires _____.

GRACE is the power that restores that _____ and _____ that man had in Eden with Him. We need to _____ for that grace, but we also need...

# Partnering with Grace – Step #2

2) _____

- God opposes _____ but gives grace to _____.

*But He gives us more and more grace (power of the Holy Spirit, to meet this evil tendency and all others fully). That is why He says, God sets Himself against the proud and haughty but gives grace [continually] to the lowly (those who are humble enough to receive it). –James 4:6 (AMPC)*

- Grace is FREE to _____.

- Humility is the only _____.

- Humility is simply…

    1. Our _____ of ourselves and of our need for God and others.

    2. An acknowledgment of where our _____ ends.

    3. A willingness to accept the truth on _____.

    4. A willingness to do it _____.

- Humility Asks…

- Humility Trusts… the _____ and that God is using the process to _____ exactly what He's _____.

# A Picture of Partnership.

In our writing journey, we will face _____, but by the _____ we overcome.

- Our partnership suffers when life's difficulties make us think...

    1) We got it _____.

    2) God's _____ us.

    3) We've somehow _____ from the promise.


- To overcome...

    1) We must DISCERN...
        - What God _____. *(A word from God can hold us when nothing else can.)*
        - Who God _____ & His _____ for you. *(His character.)*
        - Your own _____. *(Whether you are in the _____ or in the _____.)*
        - The movement of His _____ (or of its absence) within you.

    2) We must MAINTAIN...
        - _____ with Him.
        - The realization that He is our Helper, the Spirit _____, who guides us into _____. (John 16:13)

When we do His work in this_____, we begin to enter into true partnership. But there's one final component in partnering in humility with the grace of God...

# Partnering with Grace – Step #3

3) _____

*For by the grace (unmerited favor of God) given to me I warn everyone among you not to estimate and think of himself more highly that he ought [not having an exaggerated opinion of his own importance], but to rate his ability with sober judgment, each according to the degree of faith apportioned by God to him. 4 For as in one physical body we have many parts (organs, members) and all of these parts do not have the same function or use, 5 So, we numerous as we are, are one body in Christ (the Messiah) and individually we are parts of one another [mutually dependent on one another]. 6 Having gifts (faculties, talents, qualities) that differ according to the grace given us, let us use them... – **Romans 12:3-6 (AMPC)***

- Humility connects...
    - We were created to be part of _____. Humility recognizes our _____ on God and our _____ on one another.
    - Grace is only fully realized in the context of _____.

**We are created to be part of a family. Family is non-optional.**

- Your gift is from_____, but it's FOR_____, and the grace we receive from God comes most often through _____.

*As each of you has received a gift (a particular spiritual talent, a gracious divine endowment), employ it for one another as [befits] good trustees of God's many-sided grace [faithful stewards of the extremely diverse powers and gifts granted to Christians by unmerited favor]. – **1 Peter 4:10 (AMPC)***

- The _____ of the grace of God flows through _____, where one plus one equals _____.

## In Conclusion

There is no one _____ in God's Kingdom. The question is _____ has He given me? How can I partner with His grace _____ Christ's body?

**Now Let's Practice...**

# WORKSHOP TWO
## Finding Grace Mingle

***INTRODUCTION** - READING SECTION (10min) — Be sure to read all instructions and answer any questions about the activity before you start the mingle! It's sometimes fun to have soft music playing in the background for this event! (Note: If you are doing this study solo, practice this exercise the next time you are at church or with friends!)*

At this point in our study, we all have some things we're asking God about. One of the most powerful ways to partner with His grace is through learning to lean on Him and one another. This exercise will help you practice both!

1. To start, take a moment to jot down your top question for God.
2. Then, to practice partnering with others, you'll find three others to agree with in prayer—you for their requests and them, for yours.
3. To practice partnering with God's grace, as we find others to pray with, we will...
    a) Ask God for a scripture or an aspect of His character that aligns with their prayer request.
    b) Pray in agreement for their request using that scripture or attribute of God.
    c) Write down the scriptures and attributes others pray for our request.

Don't worry about whether your prayer is good enough. We're simply agreeing with what our brothers and sisters are asking for based on God's word and God's character. This is a beautiful exercise to experience how God speaks through His Body to strengthen us by what every joint supplies! (Eph. 4:16)

## WRITING SECTION (5min)

What I am asking God for: _____

_____

_____

_____

_____

## INTERACTIVE SECTION (45min)

Who Prayed with Me: _____

Scripture They Shared: _____

_____

_____

Who Prayed with Me: _____

Scripture They Shared: _____

_____

_____

Who Prayed with Me: _____

Scripture They Shared: _____

_____

_____

Who Prayed with Me: _____

Scripture They Shared: _____

_____

# Others I Prayed For:

NAME: _____

Prayer Request: _____

Scripture I Prayed for Them: _____

_____

_____

_____

NAME: _____

Prayer Request: _____

Scripture I Prayed for Them: _____

_____

_____

_____

NAME: _____

Prayer Request: _____

Scripture I Prayed for Them: _____

_____

_____

_____

NAME: _____

Prayer Request: _____

Scripture I Prayed for Them: _____

_____

_____

_____

# LESSON THREE
## *Grace to be Untethered: An Invitation to Dance*

### By Laurel Thomas

*An invitation to dance is both unique and personal freedom as a creative. Discover a world of wonder ready to be expressed in words. There's no need to fear. He promised we'd never dance/create alone!*

**PROVERBS 8:22-30 (The Passion Translation) – Creation**

*In the beginning, I was there (Spirit of wisdom, Jesus) … Before the ocean depths were poured out and before there were any glorious fountains overflowing with water,*

*I was there—dancing.*

*Even before one mountain had been sculpted or one hill raised up, I was already there—dancing. When I set in place the pillars of the earth and spoke the degrees of the seas, commanding waves so they wouldn't overstep their boundaries,*

*I was there—close to the Creator's side as His master artist.*

**What does creative worship look like on us?**
Don't wait to be invited! You're already welcome to a fountain that He placed inside of you before the creation of earth itself.

# PROTECTING AND CARING FOR THE TEMPLE – US!

He delivered and saved and called us with a holy calling—a calling that leads to a *set-apart life of purpose*, not because of our works, but because of *His own purpose and grace.* **2 Timothy 1:9 – Amplified**

- **Wisdom is THE GATEKEEPER. (Jesus, the Spirit of Wisdom)**
  He became to us wisdom from God, righteousness, sanctification, and redemption. **I Corinthians 1:30**

- **We're connected to Him!**

May you be filled with the knowledge of His will in all spiritual wisdom and understanding, so that you walk in a manner worthy of the Lord, to please Him in all respects, bearing fruit in every good work, and increasing in the knowledge of God... (**Colossians 1:9**)

# ACCESSING Wisdom:

**LISTENING** – Journaling, prayer, etc.

LISTEN, for I will speak noble things, and the opening of my lips will reveal right things. **Proverbs 8:6** *(NASB)*

### WHY LISTEN?

**Proverbs 8:34-35** (TPT) – If you wait at wisdom's doorway, longing to hear a word for every day, joy will break forth within you as you listen for what I say.

For the fountain of life pours into you every time you find Me.

**This is the secret of growing in the delight and favor of the Lord.**

**THE PASSION** – I'm calling to you, sons and daughters of Adam. Listen to me, and you will be wise…

You will find true success when you find me, for I have insights into wise plans that are designed just for you. I hold in my hand living understanding, courage, and strength. **Proverbs 8:14** *(TPT)*

## *FUELING our springs of creativity:*

**How to bring the Lord into the writing process in a practical way.**

- *Read widely.*
- *Listen to the Lord attentively – practice every day, submit all of us to all of Him. – EXAMPLES*
- *Listen to others – be teachable.*
- *Recognize the treasures that are already right beside us. Generational blessing.*
- *God-ordained friends and opportunities that may not be what we expected!*
- *Steward those treasures with diligence, with expectant faith, and by honor.*
- *Define daily action steps!*

# Interactive Exercise:

## Prayer Journaling

Use free writing, poetry, or create a scene full of sensory elements to describe something you've experienced in the last few days.

# WORKSHOP THREE
# Grace to Be Untethered: An Invitation to Dance

*Hearing the voice of God is key to our walk with God and to our writing. Join us as we explore how God speaks to you and how to cultivate that daily communication and His rhythms of rest for us.*

## Hearing God's Voice

*WRITING SECTION (10-15min)*

What's a time you felt close to God or heard from Him clearly? _____
_____
_____
_____
_____

What were some key characteristics of that moment or communication? _____
_____
_____
_____
_____

When and how do you most often hear from God?_____
_____
_____
_____
_____
_____
_____

What steps can I take to make this interaction a daily reality?_____
_____
_____
_____
_____

My Plan to Make Space for Daily Connection:_____
_____
_____
_____
_____
_____
_____
_____
_____
_____
_____
_____
_____
_____
_____

## *DISCUSSION SECTION (35min)*

- *When and how do you most often hear from God, and what are some characteristics of those times, spaces, or ways God speaks?*
- *What's a step you can take to cultivate that interaction and connection with God on a daily basis?*

# Entering His Rest

*WRITING SECTION (10-15min)*

How and when do you rest? _____
_____
_____
_____
_____
_____

What places and activities refresh your heart and mind? _____
_____
_____
_____
_____
_____

What times and spaces might you be able to set aside to establish a rhythm of rest and refilling? _____
_____
_____
_____
_____

Are there any current obstacles to your rest? _____
_____
_____
_____
_____
_____
_____

What might you be able to release and free yourself from in order to prioritize God and His rhythms of rest for you? _____
_____
_____
_____
_____
_____

My Plan to Establish Rhythms of Rest: _____
_____
_____
_____
_____
_____
_____
_____
_____
_____
_____
_____

## *DISCUSSION SECTION (35min)*

- *How and when do you rest and what kinds of things refresh you?*
- *When and how can you set aside time and space to rest, if you don't already?*
- *What is your biggest obstacle/obstacles in establishing a regular rhythm of rest and how might you overcome them?*

# Friends Met @ Meeting #3

NAME:_____

EMAIL:_____PHONE:_____

NOTES:_____

_____

_____

_____


NAME:_____

EMAIL:_____PHONE:_____

NOTES:_____

_____

_____

_____


NAME:_____

EMAIL:_____PHONE:_____

NOTES:_____

_____

_____

_____


NAME:_____

EMAIL:_____PHONE:_____

NOTES:_____

_____

_____

_____

# LESSON FOUR

## Comfort for the Writer's Soul: God's Word for God's Writers Today

### By Janice Buswell

*The world is a chaotic place, and writing in the middle of the tumult can feel daunting. How can you complete the call of God amidst the chaos? Join us this session to see what God is speaking in this season to His writers.*

## What is God Saying to Us as Writers Today?

### Isaiah 40 *(NKJV)*

¹ "Comfort, yes, comfort My people!" Says your God. ² "Speak comfort to Jerusalem, and cry out to her, that her warfare is ended, that her iniquity is pardoned; for she has received from the LORD's hand double for all her sins."

_____
_____
_____
_____

- *Brothers and sisters, I do not consider myself yet to have taken hold of it. But one thing I do: Forgetting what is behind and straining toward what is ahead, I press on toward the goal to win the prize for which God has called me heavenward in Christ Jesus. – Philippians 3:13-14 (NIV)*

- *"Forget the former things; do not dwell on the past. See, I am doing a new thing! Now it springs up; do you not perceive it? I am making a way in the wilderness and streams in the wasteland. The wild animals honor me, the jackals and the owls, because I provide water in the wilderness and streams in the wasteland, to give drink to my people, my chosen..." - Isaiah 43:18-20 (NIV)*

³ The voice of one crying in the wilderness: "Prepare the way of the LORD; Make straight in the desert a highway for our God. ⁴ Every valley shall be exalted and every mountain and hill brought low; The crooked places shall be made straight and the rough places smooth; ⁵ The glory of the LORD shall be revealed, and all flesh shall see *it* together; For the mouth of the LORD has spoken."

⁶ The voice said, "Cry out!" And he said, "What shall I cry?"
"All flesh *is* grass, and all its loveliness *is* like the flower of the field.

⁷ The grass withers, the flower fades, because the breath of the LORD blows upon it; Surely the people *are* grass. ⁸ The grass withers, the flower fades, but the word of our God stands forever."

_____
_____
_____
_____
_____

⁹ O Zion, You who bring good tidings, Get up into the high mountain; O Jerusalem, You who bring good tidings, lift up your voice with strength, lift *it* up, be not afraid; Say to the cities of Judah, "Behold your God!"

_____
_____
_____
_____
_____

¹⁰ Behold, the Lord GOD shall come with a strong *hand,* and His arm shall rule for Him; Behold, His reward *is* with Him, and His work before Him. ¹¹ He will feed His flock like a shepherd; He will gather the lambs with His arm, and carry *them* in His bosom, *and* gently lead those who are with young.

_____
_____
_____
_____
_____

¹² Who has measured the waters in the hollow of His hand, measured heaven with a span and calculated the dust of the earth in a measure? Weighed the mountains in scales and the hills in a balance?

_____
_____
_____
_____
_____

¹³ Who has directed the Spirit of the LORD, or *as* His counselor has taught Him? ¹⁴ With whom did He take counsel, and *who* instructed Him, and taught Him in the path of justice? Who taught Him knowledge, and showed Him the way of understanding?

_____
_____
_____
_____
_____

¹⁵ Behold, the nations *are* as a drop in a bucket, and are counted as the small dust on the scales; Look, He lifts up the isles as a very little thing. ¹⁶ And Lebanon *is* not sufficient to burn, nor its beasts sufficient for a burnt offering. ¹⁷ All nations before Him *are* as nothing, and they are counted by Him less than nothing and worthless.

_____
_____
_____

¹⁸ To whom then will you liken God? Or what likeness will you compare to Him? ¹⁹ The workman molds an image, the goldsmith overspreads it with gold, and the silversmith casts silver chains. ²⁰ Whoever *is* too impoverished for *such* a contribution chooses a tree *that* will not rot; He seeks for himself a skillful workman to prepare a carved image *that* will not totter.

_____
_____
_____
_____

²¹ Have you not known? Have you not heard? Has it not been told you from the beginning? Have you not understood from the foundations of the earth? ²² *It is* He who sits above the circle of the earth, and its inhabitants *are* like grasshoppers, who stretches out the heavens like a curtain, and spreads them out like a tent to dwell in. ²³ He brings the princes to nothing; He makes the judges of the earth useless.

²⁴ Scarcely shall they be planted, scarcely shall they be sown, scarcely shall their stock take root in the earth, when He will also blow on them, and they will wither, and the whirlwind will take them away like stubble.

²⁵ "To whom then will you liken Me, or *to whom* shall I be equal?" says the Holy One. ²⁶ Lift up your eyes on high, and see who has created these *things,* who brings out their host by number; He calls them all by name, by the greatness of His might and the strength of *His* power; Not one is missing.

²⁷ Why do you say, O Jacob, and speak, O Israel, "My way is hidden from the LORD, and my just claim is passed over by my God"? ²⁸ Have you not known? Have you not heard? The everlasting God, the LORD, the Creator of the ends of the earth, neither faints nor is weary. His understanding is unsearchable.

²⁹ He gives power to the weak, and to *those who have* no might He increases strength. ³⁰ Even the youths shall faint and be weary, and the young men shall utterly fall, ³¹ but those who wait on the LORD shall renew *their* strength; They shall mount up with wings like eagles, they shall run and not be weary, they shall walk and not faint.

# WORKSHOP FOUR
# Comfort for the Writer's Soul: God's Word for God's Writers Today

*J*oin us as we explore our response and develop some concrete steps to apply God's powerful message from Isaiah 40!

WRITING SECTION (40min) - This workshop is unique. The writing section carries all the way through to the last question on page 46. When you've answered all the "Tying It Together" questions, you will move into a time of discussion.

## Clarifying the Vision

What past failure or present failing do you need to trust to the Lord?

**Preoccupation with the past obscures our vision of the future.** God is getting ready to move. Let's make space for Him to do all He's planned to do through us!

Are there any "urgent" distractions currently in your life?

What word(s) has God spoken to you?

Do you have any scriptures that support that word/those words? If not, pause and ask the Father for one!

What scriptures or word from God do you need to grow your faith in?

## Ways We Grow Faith

1) **Hearing**. Faith comes by hearing. This is why it's important to regularly read aloud or pray out loud and declare the words and scriptures God's given you. Faith comes by hearing and hearing by the Word of God. (Rom. 10:17)
2) **Seeing**. Put what God has said to you somewhere you can see it daily. Where there is no vision the people perish. (Pro. 29:18) Write the vision and make it plain so that he who reads it may run with it. (Hab. 2:2)
3) **Prayer**. Prayer and journaling are excellent ways to grow your faith as you talk to God regularly about the words and scriptures He's given you. "Ask and it will be given to you; seek and you will find; knock and the door will be opened to you. For everyone who asks receives; he who seeks finds; and to him who knocks, the door will be opened." (Mat. 7:7-8)

4) **Imagination**. Spending time imagining what the fulfillment of God's word and call on your life will look like is a great way to grow your faith. Imagining engages your heart and mind prayerfully and playfully in planning and preparation to see that God-dream become a reality. So many dreams never come into being because they were forgotten or neglected. As a man thinks in His heart so is He. (Pro.s 23:7)
5) **Action**. Faith without works is dead. (Jam. 2:26) What small step can you take today or this week toward the word God's given you?

## Remembering Who God Is (And Who You Are Because of Him!)

What aspects of God's character do you need to remember?

What verses remind you of who He's promised to be for you?

In what aspects of this world and life do you need to recognize God's sovereign control?

Is there a word God's spoken about you that you're struggling to believe?

What can you do to change that belief?

Have you viewed anything as bigger than God or as capable of stopping His plans for you?

What alternate source have you unintentionally been relying on for blessing in your life?

What world event do you need to lift to God in prayer—and leave at His feet when prayer time is over?

## Staying In Step with God

Where might you need to shift your focus so you and your story can be ready for God's move?

What things should be reduced or removed?

What things should be added?

**Timing is about staying in step with God**.
Where is God calling you to take action?



Where is God calling you to patiently wait and prepare?



## Changing Our Strength

Are there areas of your life you feel God has forgotten?



Where do you need to wait on the Lord in prayer, worship, and His word and receive His strength?



**Changing our strength is about trust.** When we trust God, we rely on His strength instead of ours. The more we know Him, the more we'll trust Him. Getting to know someone takes some intentional time and energy and a choice to be involved with them and to let them be involved with you.

# Tying It All Together - *Draw from your answers to the previous questions to answer the discussion questions below. Following these four steps will help you untether from what's held you back!*

Questions:
1) What's been your biggest distraction from the Lord and His comfort in this season? Is it a failing, a demand on your time, a world event, an obstacle, or alternate source of strength?
2) What do you need to surrender and trust to God?
3) Where does your focus need to shift?
4) A. Where and how will you strengthen your faith?
   B. What characteristic of God will you get to know better in order to change from your strength to His?

Answers:

1) Problem: _____
_____
_____

2) Point of Surrender: _____
_____
_____

3) Perspective Shift: _____
_____
_____

4-A.) Plan to Grow Faith: _____
_____
_____

4-B.) Characteristic of God to Embrace: _____
_____
_____

## *DISCUSSION SECTION (40min)*

- *Share a 2-minute synopsis of your problem, point of surrender, perspective shift, plan to grow faith, and characteristic of God to embrace!*

# Friends Met @ Meeting #4

NAME:_____

EMAIL:_____PHONE:_____

NOTES:_____

_____

_____

_____

NAME:_____

EMAIL:_____PHONE:_____

NOTES:_____

_____

_____

_____

NAME:_____

EMAIL:_____PHONE:_____

NOTES:_____

_____

_____

_____

NAME:_____

EMAIL:_____PHONE:_____

NOTES:_____

_____

_____

_____

## LESSON FIVE
# Grace for Identity – Unearthing Treasure in Ourselves through Community

### By Laurel Thomas

*Join us as we discover the uniqueness of Him in ourselves and in each other. Uncover unexpected pearls that have been inside us all along!*

## PERSONAL IDENTITY:

What does gatekeeper look like *on me*?

**PSALM 33:9 (The Passion Translation)**

*You breathed words and worlds were birthed.*

**What worlds are birthed through our words? SELAH! Stop and think about this!**

His plan is to propel us and our creative gift. In the meantime, we become part of a bigger whole.

## DEAL BREAKERS:

Fear – Fear is the granddaddy of all that tries to separate us from His goodness.

Dishonor – Based in poverty and *not enough*. Your success doesn't diminish mine.

Isolation – Based on fear and even pride that we need to do this on our own.

## I PETER 2:9 – OUR IDENTITY

The Passion Translation – You are God's chosen treasure—***priests who are kings***, a spiritual "nation" set apart as God's devoted ones ... to *broadcast His glorious wonders throughout the world.*

*Writing is a priestly thing, connecting people to God. To connect people to His heart through words. Don't give up!*

## WISDOM SPEAKS AT EVERY NEW GATE –

At the entrance of every portal, there she stands, READY to impart understanding, shouting aloud to all WHO ENTER. **Proverbs 8:3** *(TPT)*

## WATER BECOMING WINE! (John 2)

1. We become vessels filled with water. (OUR OWN BEST EFFORTS)

2. **Then He turns what we carry INTO WINE** – SOMETHING SWEETER THAN WE EVER EXPECTED

**WE RELEASE HIM**, HIS LIFE to an **EMPTY WORLD**.

## GLORY: God <u>demonstrated/revealed</u> on earth and in heaven.

*Glory is His plan and His will to SHOW the world who He is, through us, His believers.*

**DEFINING ELEMENTS of GLORY revealed:**

Unique and specific

Practical

Forward thinking

Bold/challenging

Revealed by FAITH, not perfection.

## SCRIPTURES:

I am the Vine, you are the branches. He who abides in me bears much fruit, for apart from Me you can do nothing. **John 15:5**

God *chose* to make known ... the mystery of Christ in you, the *confident expectation and guarantee* of realizing His glory. **Colossians 1:27**

For all have sinned and fallen short of the glory of God. **Romans 3:23**

*When we receive His sacrifice/Lordship, we no longer have to fall short of carrying and demonstrating the glory of Christ inside us.*

# Interactive Exercise:

**Locate the JOY in your writing. JOY is a signal that His glory is hidden inside! WHERE do you find your joy?**

# WORKSHOP FIVE

## *Grace for Identity – Unearthing Treasure in Ourselves through Community*

*I*dentity is something we begin to discover and fully realize in the context of community. Join us as we take the first step into this great adventure!

## Your Identity as a Writer

*WRITING SECTION (10min)*

What are some personal characteristics that are distinctively you? _____
_____
_____
_____

What are some of your most deeply held values? _____
_____
_____
_____

What are you most passionate about?_____
_____
_____
_____
_____

What's your normal way of talking?_____
_____
_____
_____
_____
_____

*DISCUSSION SECTION (20min)*
- *What are your unique characteristics, personal values, and passions?*
- *How do you normally express yourself? (Casual? Formal? Sarcastic? Whimsical?)*

These answers to these questions are clues to the distinctive voice God has given you. It's what you write. It's the way you write it. It's the way you interact with those around you, as God's glory shines through in a totally unique way.

Your story may not feel original, but the way you tell it is something that's never been seen before. And when you share the story God's given you, in the way He's created you to share it, it will touch people who may never have received that message—that encounter with His glory—in any other way.

## The Role of Community

*WRITING SECTION (10min)*

We can't truly discover who God made us to be outside of His body. A candle's light isn't recognized without being visible—without being in a room where everyone else is—for all to see. And those in the room can often see aspects of us we might never be aware of. So I have a few questions…

Who do you do life with now? _____
_____
_____
_____

Do you currently share your writing journey with anyone else? _____
_____
_____
_____
_____

How are you connected into the Body of Christ? _____
_____
_____
_____
_____

Who have you met these two days? What friends did you make? _____
_____
_____
_____
_____

Pause and ask God the following questions:

Has God highlighted certain people for you to walk with in this season? _____
_____
_____
_____
_____

Have you considered how to deepen any of these relationships?_____
_____
_____
_____
_____

*DISCUSSION SECTION (20min)*
- *What current connections/relationships do you have as a believer/writer—corporately and individually—and how deep do those connections go?*
- *How might you deepen the relationships you have?*

# Why Connection is Critical.

*READING & WRITING SECTION (15min)*

Connected writers keep writing. And they keep going. And they publish their books. And then, they get them to their readers. We've given you the keys to success these past two days. They're actually very simple though largely overlooked. **Those keys are God and His people.**

To create something of eternal impact, we must lean into the only two resources that will last for eternity. **The word of God and the souls of men.** If you've never done this, let's take a moment to formulate a connection (GROWTH) plan!

## COMMON CONNECTION OPPORTUNITIES
*(This is not exhaustive!)*

**Prayer Partners** – Don't underestimate the power of a prayer partner. They may not even be a writer or reader, but having someone who knows you, your life, and your walk, and who prays weekly for your journey (as you share it with them) will be one of the most valuable resources you ever have.

**Accountability Partners** – This can be a friend or fellow writer who is interested in your writing journey and will help keep you accountable to your goals. This is not someone who polices or disciplines you. This should be someone whose opinion matters to you. The fact that you're keeping in touch with them about your process should naturally motivate and encourage you to keep going on your journey.

**Critique Groups** – Critique groups provide an opportunity for other writers to read and give feedback on portions of your writing. Usually of a scene or a few pages. If a whole group sounds daunting, consider prayerfully seeking out a **critique partner** who is interested in you and your style of writing.

**Writers Groups** – Writers groups usually offer opportunities for fellowship and ongoing learning through speakers, critique sessions, brainstorming, etc. These groups are a great opportunity to make friends and discover critique, accountability, or prayer partners as you develop relationships in a relaxed setting.

**Conferences** – Conferences are usually half-day to multi-day events, featuring anywhere from one speaker to dozens. Conferences are a fantastic opportunity to boost your writing skills to a new level and to meet editors, publishers, agents, and other industry professionals that will help you reach the next stage of your publishing journey.

**Retreats** – The two most common types of retreats are writing retreats (focused time just to write with fellow authors) or workshopping retreats (where a professional works on a personal level with a small group of attendees to master an aspect of the writing craft). Retreats can be extremely rewarding opportunities to get more personalized feedback on your work and encouragement to write.

**Coaches** – Coaches are an excellent option if you need help knowing where to start or getting established on your writing journey. Coaches provide one-on-one interaction and feedback tailored to you and your story.

What kind of connection opportunity might fit your needs? _____
_____
_____
_____
_____

What kind of connection suits where you currently are in your writing journey?
_____
_____
_____
_____
_____
_____
_____

## *DISCUSSION SECTION (15min)*
- *Answer the two questions above.*

# LESSON SIX
## Next Steps

### By Janice Buswell

*Action begets clarity. This section is to put feet to the insights you've received from the Lord over the past five weeks. Set aside some time this week to prayerfully consider these questions and their answers. When you meet for the final time, don't forget to celebrate God's goodness with each other and your success as you take the next step of your writing journey!*

## My Next Steps

Who had God placed in my life to share my writing journey with?
_____
_____
_____
_____
_____
_____
_____
_____
_____
_____
_____
_____

When is the next time I can contact them?_____

What opportunity can I take to keep growing?
_____
_____
_____
_____
_____
_____
_____
_____
_____
_____
_____
_____
_____
_____
_____

When can I schedule my first visit? _____

My plan to connect is:_____
_____
_____
_____
_____

What is one small step you can take this week? _____
_____
_____
_____

My prayer to God:_____
_____
_____
_____
_____

God's answer to me:_____
_____
_____
_____
_____
_____
_____

# WORKSHOP SIX
## Next Steps

**Welcome, Writers!** You've completed the "Grace" course! We hope your connection to the Lord and to one another is deeper because of it. And more importantly, we pray that you've become convinced of who He's created you to be as His writer and gatekeeper of His glory.

## My Next Steps

*DISCUSSIONS SECTION (40min) – Use this week's "Next Steps" prayer reflection questions to answer the following.*
- *How do you plan to stay connected on your writing journey?*
- *How do you plan to keep growing as a writer?*
- *What is your next step toward writing your God-given story?*

*INTERACTIVE SECTION (40min) – Take time to pray for another. Feel free to use the format of the "Finding Grace Mingle."*
1) *Share and write down prayer requests.*
2) *Ask God for a scripture or attribute of His that support each request.*
3) *Pray in agreement for one another.*

*FELLOWSHIP (40min) – Enjoy and celebrate each other's gifts and progress!*

# Closing Thought

As you get ready to embark on the next stage of your journey, we encourage you to stay in touch with those the Lord has connected you to and to refer back to this workbook frequently to keep what the Lord has said fresh in your mind and heart.

May His GRACE continue to strengthen and sustain you as you throw wide the doors for His glory!

Blessings and grace,

***Janice Buswell***
*Co-Founder of Experience Writing*

# Writing Opportunities

*Keep growing with fellow writers!*

## American Christian Fiction Writers
www.acfw.com

ACFW's mission is to help you tell your stories by inspiring you to partner with God in the creative process, learn the craft, and find your audience. We're American Christian Fiction Writers, a professional organization devoted to the craft of Christian Fiction. ACFW's worldwide membership includes:

- Published Authors
- Unpublished Writers
- Editors
- Agents
- Publicists
- Librarians
- Book Club Leaders
- Reviewers

ACFW offers:

- Writing courses
- Critique groups
- Genre groups
- Local chapters
- Contests
- The premier Christian Fiction Conference
- Fellowship and encouragement
- Prayer loop

Whether you're a multi-published author or just taking the first steps in your writing career, ACFW is the place for you to learn more about the craft and expand your knowledge of the publishing industry.

# ONLINE GROUPS

## Writing Momentum
www.writingmomentum.com
*Online Community*

**Tired of writing on your own? Us too! Want HOURS of great writing training all in one spot?** Let's do it! **Join the MOVEMENT.** The **Writing Momentum Membership** is HERE – complete with online training, co-working sessions, roundtables, and more. It's like a writers' conference that never ends!

## Reedsy Live
blog.reedsy.com/live
*Online Live Sessions*

Every week we invite top professionals to share their knowledge with you live. Learn how to publish smarter, straight from the people that can help.

# CONFERENCES

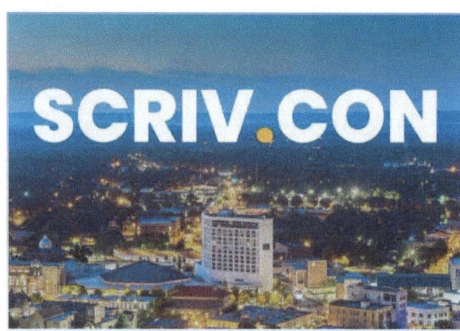

## ScrivCon
www.scrivcon.com
*Hotel Hot Springs, 305 Malvern Ave., Hot Springs, AR 71901*

ScrivCon is a content-filled event designed for writers of clean and/or Christian fiction... Presentations are focused on the craft of writing with the goal of enabling attendees to take their writing from good to great. The event is hosted yearly in November in Hot Springs, Arkansas at the Hotel Hot Springs.

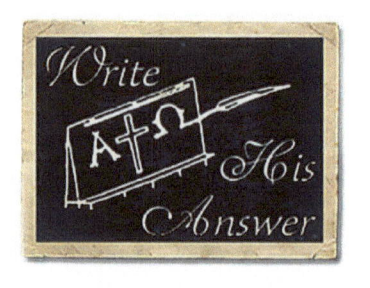

## Write His Answer
conference.writehisanswer.com/conference-details
*Online*

Write His Answer is the only totally virtual and 100% live Christian Writers Conference. Save the cost of travel and lodging as you experience all the features and more of our previous 61 in-person Colorado and Greater Philly Christian Writers Conferences. You'll be encouraged, equipped, and RENEWED (this year's theme) to take your faith-driven writing to the next level.

# About the Co-Authors

## Laurel Thomas
www.writewithlaurel.com

A former high school English teacher, Laurel Thomas loves words and their power to convey remarkable stories. *River's Call* is an award-winning novel based in the deep South. History and the fantastic mesh in her fantasy series, *When Stars Brush Earth* and *Stones of Promise*, published by Wild Rose Press. When she's not with family or roaming the halls of the Oklahoma State Bureau of Investigation as chaplain, she's doing what she loves most – crafting stories of ordinary characters rising up against impossible odds to achieve the extraordinary. Through Write Your Heart Out! and WriterCon Oklahoma City, she teaches and supports other multi-published industry professionals who equip writers for success through national conferences and weekend intensives.

## Janice Buswell
www.expwriting.com

Janice Buswell is a multi-talented communicator, speaker, *Paradoxon* series novelist, and author of the *Radical Simplicity* and *A Good Word* blogs. Her passion for stories began when she discovered they are a powerful key God uses to unlock truth in the hearts of His people. In her novels, the beauty and depth of classic literature collide with the power of modern themes in an altogether paradoxical journey. When Janice is not writing, she loves to spend her time with emerging authors in one-on-one coaching, phone calls, coffee dates, speaking engagements, and through her role as co-founder of Experience Writing and the director of their yearly conference. There are few things that make her happier than seeing writers unleashed to tell the stories only they can!

# Want More?

If you've enjoyed this study and would like more teaching and encouragement, visit expwriting.com to access additional resources and to sign up for our weekly newsletter. Or scan the QR code here!

To engage in the growing Experience Writing community, connect with us on Facebook and Instagram @expwriting.

And to meet more like-minded writers, watch for our weekly newsletter and social media channels for upcoming announcements about our yearly Experience Writing conference!

www.ingramcontent.com/pod-product-compliance
Lightning Source LLC
Chambersburg PA
CBHW042021150426
43197CB00003B/92